LITTLE
CRAFT BOOK
SERIES

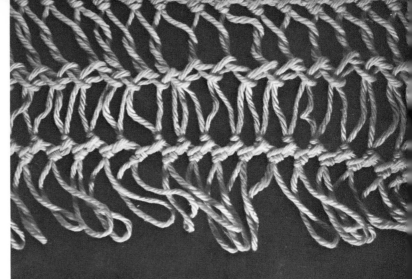

creative lace-making

with thread and yarn

By Harriet U. Fish

STERLING
PUBLISHING CO., INC.   NEW YORK
SAUNDERS OF TORONTO, Ltd., Don Mills, Canada

Oak Tree Press Co., Ltd
London & Sydney

Little Craft Book Series

Photographs by John Nelson

Drawings by Susan Henderson

Second Printing, 1973
Copyright © 1972 by Sterling Publishing Co., Inc.
419 Park Avenue South, New York, N.Y. 10016
Distributed in Canada by Saunders of Toronto, Ltd., Don Mills, Ontario
British edition published by Oak Tree Press Co., Ltd., Nassau, Bahamas
Distributed in Australia and New Zealand by Oak Tree Press Co., Ltd.,
P.O. Box 34, Brickfield Hill, Sydney 2000, N.S.W.
Distributed in the United Kingdom and elsewhere in the British Commonwealth
by Ward Lock Ltd., 116 Baker Street, London W 1
Manufactured in the United States of America
All rights reserved
Library of Congress Catalog Card No.: 72–81039
ISBN 0–8069- 5216 –4   UK 7061– 2374 –3
5217 –2

Contents

Before You Begin

Laces are open, airy products which can be created by several techniques. Each technique produces certain effects and correspondingly appropriate uses. Basically there are five different methods of producing lace: the needlepoint method, using net, tapes, cords, with thread and needle to fasten them together; the bobbin method, weaving by numerous threaded bobbins, twisted and whirled in a pattern on a pillow; the knitted method; the tatted method; and the crocheted method. Each of these techniques involves an individual set of instructions, stitches, patterns and equipment.

The word "lace," derived from the Latin word *laqueus*, means noose or snare. Noose, in turn, is "a loop with a running knot that binds closer the more it is drawn." This is certainly true of the crochet loop which makes one kind of lace—Hairpin Lace. This book deals with Hairpin Lace, usually made on a hairpin-shaped frame. This is crocheted lace with variations limited only by your own imagination. You can create useful and attractive lacy products with a relatively small investment in equipment and materials, and with a modest amount of time, effort and skill. All you have to do is master the few basic rules and stitches.

The basic stitches, called loop (lp), yarn over (yo), chain (ch), single crochet (sc), double crochet (dc), and half double crochet (hdc), are the stitches most used in this type of lace-making. (The instructions will refer to the stitches by their letter abbreviations. The * means repeat from that point.) The projects you create can be large or small, fine or coarse—from afghans, stoles and shawls, to wall hangings, curtains and floral decorations. Even a wedding dress, made 50 years ago and handed down as an heirloom, is the product of the Hairpin Lace process. Use any combinations of the basic stitches that you know, such as the Popcorn, Star, Shell and Cluster stitches, to further enhance your Hairpin Lace projects. You may even, hopefully, develop patterns of your own for unique and individual, one-of-a-kind Hairpin Lace creations.

Illus. 1. You can make attractive Hairpin Lace with any of these materials. Use different textures and unusual colors for especially creative effects.

Materials

Almost any kind and size of yarn, worsted, twine, string, cord, rope, or thread, made of cotton, linen, wool, silk, metal, nylon, or artificial fibres, is suitable for making Hairpin Lace. However, you need a few precautions. Select a material whose shape, in cross-section, is round. Because most ribbons and other flat, lifeless materials usually do not work up well, use materials that have some firmness and body to them. Raffia and other strawlike materials, which have some stiffness, are an exception, and the twist which develops during the Hairpin Lace process actually seems to enhance them. Other slippery, limp materials are not as easy for the beginner to use. With patience, practice, and experience, though, you will be able to produce a

5

TABLE I

American			K/10¼	J/10	I/9	H/8	H/8	G/6	F/5	E/4	D/3	C/2	B/1	
English			2	3	4	5	6	7	8	9	10	11	12	13	14
Continental metric		7½	7	6½	6	5½	5	4½	4	3½	3¼	3/2¾	2½	2¼	2

luscious fabric using chenille and velvety yarns even though they have less body. For small projects, use left-overs and odds and ends.

If you are going to buy crochet cottons, remember that the higher the number, the smaller the thread diameter. Size 30, then, is thicker than size 80. Wools are usually measured by plys (the number of strands of wool). The more plys, the larger the diameter of the yarn. So, 4-ply wool is thicker than 2-ply.

Equipment

Crochet Hook

NOTE: Crochet hook sizes in this book are American. Convert to English and Continental metric sizes as shown in Table I.

Although crochet hooks are available almost universally, sizing methods vary. In metal hooks, the smaller the number, the larger the hook end. A high number such as 14 would be very small and fine. In plastic hooks, the sizing is from D to J, and D is smaller than J; in aluminum hooks, the sizing is from B to K, and B is smaller than K. The smallest aluminum hooks are comparable to the largest of the metal hooks.

Illus. 2 (below left). If you use fine thread on too wide a frame setting, the result, shown here, is flimsy and unattractive.

Illus. 3 (below right). If you use coarse yarn on too narrow a frame setting and with too small a hook, the result is lumpy and coarse.

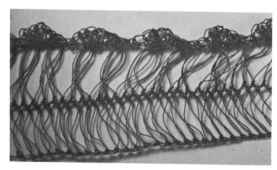

Hairpin Lace Frames

The Hairpin Lace equipment is known by several terms—frame, fork, loom. All of these are looms in the sense that fabric is made on them. The three words are, however, used interchangeably by lace-makers and equipment manufacturers.

Hairpin frames are available in knit and weaving shops where you would buy crochet hooks and yarn-type materials. There are several styles with different width settings. The diameter of the material you use has a definite relationship to the size of the crochet hook and the width of the Hairpin Lace frame. The crochet hook and the frame can be too large for the size of the material, or the

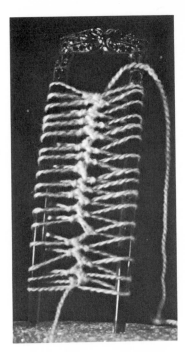

Illus. 4. This Victorian tortoise-shell hairpin is more elaborate than most frames available today.

frame can be too narrow for the size of the hook and material. For smaller diameter yarn, you must use a small hook and narrow setting on the frame.

In the Victorian period, when Hairpin Lacemaking was at its peak, the ladies actually used their large bone hairpins for frames (see Illus. 4). Today, you can use any of several different types of frames.

The Hairpin fork in Illus. 5, the older style loom, is shaped like a hairpin and has two points like a fork. Open at one end and rounded at the other, the Hairpin fork has a spacer bar which slides up and down to keep the distance between the prongs even. Remove this bar when you complete your work. This type of loom is a

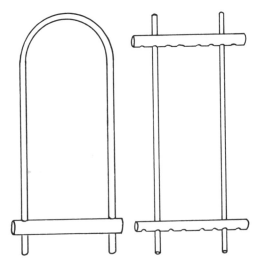

Illus. 5. Hairpin fork (left) and Hairpin crochet frame or fork (right).

7

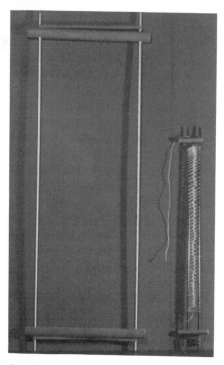

work like any commercial frame. To make a frame for very fine lace—using small diameter thread and a tiny crochet hook—purchase a set of small-sized, metal double-ended sock needles for knitting (they come four in a set). Decide the width you wish to use, and drill holes the size of the needles in two pieces of $\frac{1}{4}''$ dowelling, making sure that both pieces are drilled identically, so the rods will be parallel. Do the same thing with the second pair of needles, but space the holes differently, so that you have two Hairpin Lace frames for fine work.

If you wish to have a longer and larger frame for afghan and stole work, buy welding rod or aluminum rod $\frac{1}{8}''$ or $\frac{3}{16}''$ in diameter and do the same thing as for the smaller frame, using dowelling large enough to accommodate the evenly spaced holes. (For more detail, see page 44.)

If, for any reason, the rods or prongs slip out of the holes in either the hand-made or commercial frames, wind an elastic band round the metal ends outside of the dowelling or bar (see Illus. 6). Also, be sure the ends of the prongs and rods are smooth, so they do not scratch or catch your yarn or thread.

The rule for success in scale in making Hairpin Lace is to set the frame *wide* for coarse or heavy materials, and *close* together for fine materials. You will notice that the wider the fork, the more awkward is the rotating motion you use and the more room is necessary for the lace-making process.

fixed size, so you must have several of varying widths if you are interested in more than one size lace.

Although the Hairpin crochet frame or fork in Illus. 5 does not actually have prongs as a fork does, the points are still called prongs. This frame is composed of two metal side rails and two plastic or wooden bars which slide up and down and equalize the spacing as you work. The Hairpin crochet frame is adjustable, and on it you can make lace in eight different widths from $\frac{1}{2}''$ to $4''$ in $\frac{1}{2}''$ intervals.

You can also make your own Hairpin Lace frame, in any size you wish, which will look and

Basic Stitches for Hairpin Lace

American	English
yarn over (yo)	wool round hook
chain (ch)	chain
slip stitch (sl st)	single crochet
single crochet (sc)	double crochet
half double crochet (hdc)	half treble crochet
double crochet (dc)	treble crochet

Illus. 7.

You must be familiar with the basic crochet stitches before you can make crocheted Hairpin Lace. Start with a medium-sized hook (F or G) and at least a 2-ply or, preferably, a 4-ply worsted or yarn. Of course, large-sized hooks work with fine thread, but the result is unattractive and flimsy. Using a small hook with large yarn is not as easy to do, but is equally as unattractive and bunchy. Gauge your thread and crochet hook compatably. After a few stitches, you can tell which change should be made, if any, for the result to be useful, attractive and worth your time to make.

Make the loop first.

Step 1: Grasp the thread near the end between the thumb and forefinger of your left hand. Lap the long thread over the short thread (supply thread over end) and hold the loop in place between your thumb and forefinger (Illus. 7).

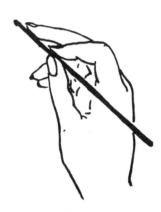

Illus. 8.

Step 2: With your right hand, take hold of the flat bar of the hook as you would a pencil. Then, bring your middle finger forward to rest near the tip of the hook (Illus. 8). Holding the hook this way enables you to control the position of the hook end.

9

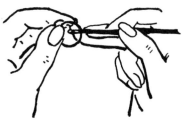

Illus. 9.

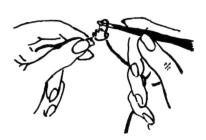

Illus. 10.

Step 3: Put your hook through the loop, catch the long end of the supply thread (attached to the ball of yarn), and draw it through (Illus. 9).

Step 4: Do not remove the hook from the thread loop. Pull the short end and supply thread in opposite directions to bring the loop close, but not too tight, round the end of the hook (Illus. 10).

Hold the thread with your left hand.

Step 5: Measure with your eye about 4″ of the supply thread from the loop on the hook. At about this point, insert the thread between your ring and little fingers with the palm of your hand facing up (Illus. 11).

Step 6: Bring the thread towards the back, under your little and ring fingers, over the middle finger, and under the forefinger towards the thumb (Illus. 12).

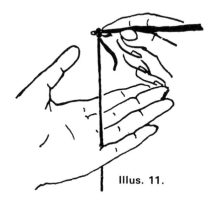

Illus. 11.

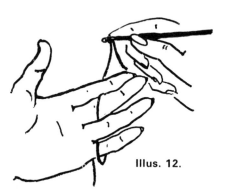

Illus. 12.

10

Step 7: Grasp the hook and loop between the thumb and forefinger of your left hand. Gently pull the supply thread so that it lies around your fingers firmly but not tightly (Illus. 13). This gives you control.

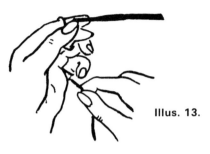

Illus. 13.

Step 8: Catch the knot of the loop between your thumb and forefinger. Bend your middle finger in such a way as to regulate the tension of the thread and regulate the ring and little fingers to prevent the thread from moving too freely (Illus. 14). As you practice you will become familiar with the correct position for you. Keep in mind that the motion of the hook in the right hand and the thread in the left hand should be easy and smooth. One of the most common faults of beginners is to crochet either too tightly or too loosely.

Chain Stitch (ch)

You already have one loop on your hook.

Step 1: Pass your hook under the thread and catch the supply thread with the hook (Illus. 15). This is called "thread over" or "yarn over." Draw the thread through the loop on the hook. This makes one chain (ch). If the hook does not slide easily, the thread is too tight.

Step 2: Repeat Step 1 until you have as many chain stitches as you need. One loop always remains on the hook (Illus. 16). Always keep the thumb and forefinger of your left hand near the stitch on which you are working. Practice making chains until they are even in size and lie flat, all in the same direction. If too much light shows through each loop and it looks loose, the hook is too large for the diameter of the yarn.

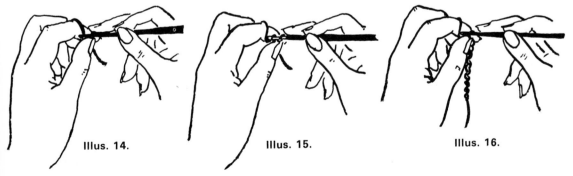

Illus. 14.   Illus. 15.   Illus. 16.

Single Crochet (sc)

Step 1: Make a foundation chain of 20 stitches to use for practice (ch 20). To begin the row, insert the hook from the front, under the two top threads (front and back) of the second chain (ch) from the hook (Illus. 17).

Illus. 17.

Step 2: Catch the thread with the hook (yarn over) (Illus. 18) and draw through the stitch (st). There are now two loops on the hook (Illus. 19).

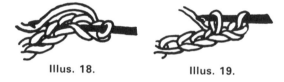

Illus. 18.   Illus. 19.

Step 3: Yarn over and draw it through both loops. One loop remains on the hook. You have now completed one single crochet (sc) (Illus. 20).

Illus. 20.

Step 4: For the next single crochet (sc), insert the hook under two top threads of the next stitch (st) and proceed as before (repeat Steps 2 and 3). Repeat until you have made a single crochet in every stitch (20 sc). At the end of the row of single crochets, chain 1 (ch 1) (Illus. 21). Turn your work so that the reverse side is facing you (Illus. 22).

Illus. 21.   Illus. 22.

For the second, third and however many remaining rows you wish to crochet, insert the hook from the front under the two top threads (front and back) of the second stitch from the hook (first stitch on the previous row). Then, repeat Steps 2, 3 and 4 in the directions for the first row.

At the end of the last row, do not make a turning chain. Clip the thread about 3″ from your work, bring the loose end through the one loop remaining on the hook and pull tightly (Illus. 23). Now you have completed a practice piece of single crochet.

NOTE: In all crochet, it is customary to pick up both of the two top threads (front and back) of

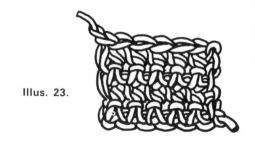

Illus. 23.

12

every stitch unless otherwise directed. When you only pick up the back stitch, the result is called rib stitch.

In crochet, you must add a certain number of chain stitches at the end of every row. Then, turn the work so that the reverse side is facing you. You have noticed that in the single crochet, you use only one chain for turning. The number of turning chains depends upon the stitch with which you intend to begin the next row. The exact number will usually be given in the directions. The turning chain always counts as the first stitch, except in single crochet where ch 1 only raises the work to position, but does not count as the first stitch.

Double Crochet (dc)

Step 1: Make a foundation chain of 20 stitches (ch 20) for a practice piece. To begin the row, yarn over (yo) and insert the hook from the front under the two top threads of the fourth chain (ch) from hook (Illus. 24). Yarn over (yo) and draw the thread through the stitch (st). There are now three loops on the hook.

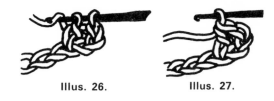

Illus. 24.

Illus. 25.

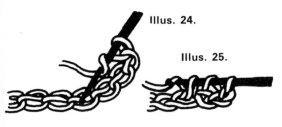

Step 2: Yarn over (Illus. 25) and draw through two loops. Two loops remain on hook (Illus. 26).

Step 3: Thread over again and draw through the two remaining loops (one loop remains on

Illus. 26.   Illus. 27.

the hook). You have now completed one double crochet (Illus. 27). For the next double crochet (dc), yarn over, insert the hook from the front under the two top threads of the next stitch and proceed as above. Repeat until you have made a double crochet in every chain.

Step 4: At the end of the row, chain three (ch 3) (Illus. 28) and turn. The three chain stitches count as the first double crochet (dc) of the next row.

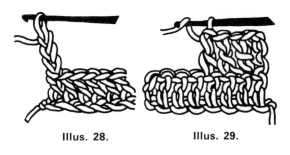

Illus. 28.   Illus. 29.

To begin the second, third and remaining rows, yarn over, insert the hook from the front under the two top threads of the fifth stitch from the hook (second stitch on the previous row). Proceed as above (Illus. 29).

Finish off at the end of your desired length by cutting the thread 3″ from the last double crochet. Bring the end through the loop and pull tightly.

13

Half Double Crochet (hdc)

Make the stitch known as half double crochet (hdc) by first repeating Step 1 of double crochet. At that point, there are three loops on the hook. Then, yarn over and draw through all three loops at once (Illus. 30). In half double crochet, chain 2 (ch 2) to turn.

Illus. 30.

Slip Stitch (sl st)

Use slip stitch only for joining or when an invisible stitch is required. When the directions say join, always use a slip stitch.

Step 1: Insert the hook from the front through the two top threads of the stitch (Illus. 31).

Step 2: Yarn over and with one motion, draw through the stitch and the loop on the hook. One loop remains on the hook (Illus. 32).

Increase or Decrease

If you are instructed to increase, make two stitches in one stitch. Each time you do this, you make an extra stitch on that row.

Decrease in Single Crochet

Step 1: Complete the single crochet to the point where two loops remain on the hook. Keep the two loops on the hook and insert the hook from under the two top threads of the next stitch. Yarn over and draw through the stitch. There are now three loops on the hook (Illus. 33).

Step 2: Yarn over and draw through the three loops at once. One loop remains on the hook. You have now worked two single crochets together and there is one stitch less on the row (Illus. 34).

Illus. 33.

Illus. 34.

Illus. 31.

Illus. 32.

Decrease in Double Crochet

Step 1: Make a double crochet to the point where there are two loops on the hook. Keep the two loops on the hook, yarn over, and insert the hook from the front under the two top threads of the next stitch. Yarn over and draw through the stitch. There are now four loops on the hook (Illus. 35).

Illus. 35.

Step 2: Yarn over again and draw through two loops. Three loops remain on the hook (Illus. 36).

Illus. 36.

Step 3: Yarn over and draw through the three loops. One loop remains on the hook (Illus. 37). You have now worked two double crochets together and there is one less stitch on the row.

Illus. 37.

Edge on Handkerchief

Now that you have mastered the basic crochet stitches and understand the size relationship of material to hook to patterns, apply it to the Hairpin Lace technique. The first Hairpin Lace was edging on dainty handkerchiefs as in Illus. 38.

Materials: One hemstitched handkerchief (hemstitching is a method of hemming that involves drawing threads from the handkerchief at the hemline and then uniformly stitching several of the loose perpendicular stitches together); one ball of white or colored cotton tatting thread, #30 or finer; size 8 metal crochet hook; Hairpin Lace frame, set at $\frac{1}{2}''$.

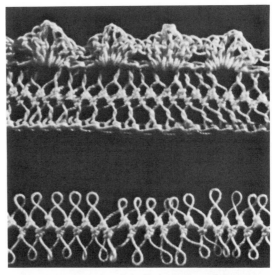

Illus. 38. Attach the plain Hairpin Lace (shown on the bottom) to a handkerchief and then add the dainty shell edging (pictured on the top).

Illus. 39. Hairpin Lace flowers are fun and easy to make. Since they do not have to be realistic, be artistic and create lovely flowers of wild and unusual colors.

Illus. 40. After you have "grown" your flowers—with leaves and stems, of course—make a permanent bouquet by gluing them to a plaque. Instructions are on pages 26–28.

Illus. 41. What safer way could there be to carry your groceries home than this rip-proof Hairpin Lace grocery bag?

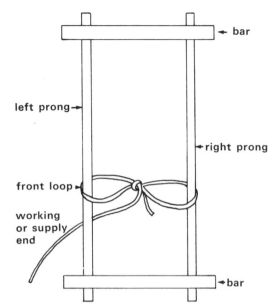

Illus. 42. Parts of an adjustable Hairpin crochet loom or frame.

left prong →

→ right prong

front loop →

working or supply end →

← bar

← bar

the rear of the work and hold it in your left hand as you would for crocheting (see page 10).

The lace edging shown in Illus. 38 has a single crochet center.

Step 1: Insert the hook under the front strand of the left-of-center loop and pull a thread through (one loop on the hook). Chain 1 stitch (still 1 loop on hook).

Step 2: Rotate the frame one-half turn from right to left towards you, winding a loop from the supply around the left prong of the frame, which now becomes the right prong (Illus. 43). To do this, either remove the hook from the loop and replace it back in the loop from the opposite side, after the loom is rotated, or pass the shank of the hook through the middle of the loom, to the the other side as it is rotated. If you are using a hairpin without any bar, you can throw the hook from side to side without removing it from the loop. Simply pass it through the open end of the hairpin. With the hook in the remaining stitch, pass the hook under the front of the loop on

Work sc around all four edges of the handkerchief, having about 12 sc to the inch, and remembering to do 3 sc in each corner stitch. End off. Count sc stitches. Hopefully, you have an even number.

Make enough Hairpin Lace loops on the frame to match the number of sc along the edges of the handkerchief. If this is an even number, the pattern following will work out evenly without adjustments.

Hold the frame in your left hand; loop yarn round the frame and tie a secure knot in the center, leaving a 3″ end for use later if necessary. Always keep the supply or working end of the yarn at

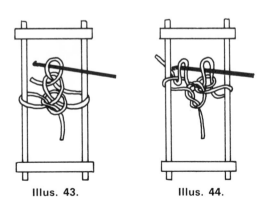

Illus. 43.   **Illus. 44.**

18

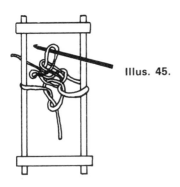

Illus. 45.

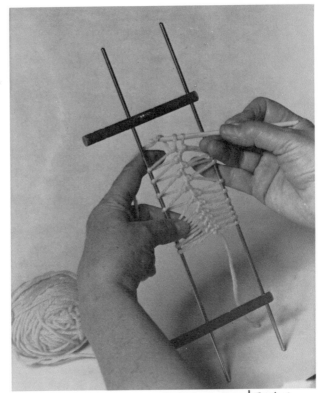

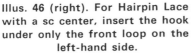

Illus. 46 (right). For Hairpin Lace with a sc center, insert the hook under only the front loop on the left-hand side.

the left-hand side. Pick up the thread with the hook (yo) and bring it through the loop (two loops on hook) (Illus. 44).

Step 3: Pick up thread (yo) and pull through both loops (Illus. 45).

Repeat Steps 2 and 3 until you have made as many loops as sc stitches on the handkerchief. Remember that when a pattern calls for a certain number of loops, you must have the designated number of loops on *each* side of the loom. 20 loops means 20 right and 20 left.

If the frame fills up and you still need a longer strip, slip the bar from the bottom of the loom and take off all but three or four loops on each side of the loom. Replace the bar and roll up the loops that have been removed and fasten them with a stitch holder to keep them from twisting and stretching.

To fasten off, always leave an 8″ strand of thread at the end of each strip. Pull it through the last loop of the single crochet to keep the strip from unravelling.

Illus. 47. Even your
first endeavors should
look like this.
Hairpin Lace is not
difficult to make at all!

Now, remove the lace from the frame, being careful to keep the twist in the loops.

Step 4: Keeping the twist in all the loops, join the thread to the first sc in one corner of the handkerchief and sc each loop of lace to each sc on the edges of the handkerchief, remembering to fasten three loops at each corner so it will lie flat. Fasten off.

Step 5: Join the thread to the outside of the Hairpin Lace loops and, again, keeping the twist in all the loops, do one row of sc all round.

Step 6: For the second row, do a shell stitch along this sc edge of lace. Make the shell stitch as follows: * 3 dc in first space between loops, ch 3, 3 dc all in same space. This is a shell. Skip 3 spaces between loops and repeat from * around the handkerchief. Remember to make two shells at each corner.

Try other crocheted edgings with this fine thread to use on blouses, slips, baby clothes and table linen. This is true Hairpin Lace.

20

Wall Decorations

Bell Cord

Materials: one adjustable Hairpin Lace frame, set at 2″, or a 2″-wide fork; size H or larger crochet hook; two balls of contrasting sisal cord (green and natural were used for the bell cord in Illus. 49); two yards of contrasting (orange) $\frac{1}{2}″$ grosgrain ribbon (or 1″ doubled for extra rigidity); felt of a blending color (green): one piece for the top, $2\frac{1}{4}″ \times 1″$, and two pieces for the bottom, $2\frac{1}{4}″ \times 1\frac{1}{4}″$, trimmed so that the bottom edge is $\frac{1}{2}″$ narrower than the top edge (Illus. 48); one 1″ metal ring for top hanging; one 2″ bell for the bottom.

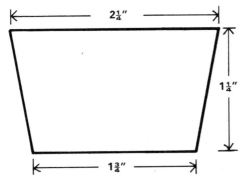

$2\frac{1}{4}″$

$1\frac{1}{4}″$

$1\frac{3}{4}″$

Illus. 48. Trim the felt for the bottom edge like this.

Illus. 49 (right). Make this bell cord for an unusual housegift for a friend—in almost less time than it would take to bake a cake!

Step 1: To make the bell cord in Illus. 49, single crochet one strip of Hairpin Lace (make a strip with a single crochet center) with 40 loops on each side, working the two colors together simultaneously. Leave at least 4″ ends at the beginning and end.

Step 2: Remove the strip from the frame and place it on a flat surface. Without keeping the twist in the loops, thread the grosgrain ribbon through the loops, using one yard for each side. The ribbon in Illus. 49 is 1″ ribbon folded lengthwise.

Step 3: Hand stitch the top piece of felt, folding it lengthwise at the top to catch the center sc of the lace and the ends of the ribbon. Tack the metal ring to the center top. To shape the bottom pieces of felt, hand stitch them one on each side of the lace, widest side up towards the sc and the ribbon. Tack the bell to the center of the bottom of the felt.

The bell cord is an unusual gift or addition to your own home.

Wall Hanging

Materials: two balls of hemp rope in two contrasting colors; Hairpin Lace frame, set at 3″; size H crochet hook; 12 pieces of 1″ veneer of cedar, birch, redwood or other wood; large, strong stapler; 12 ceramic beads (optional).

Sand the edges of the veneer and set the pieces aside.

Step 1: To make the smart-looking wall hanging in Illus. 52, work five lace strips—two of one color and three of the other—with 34 loops on each side.

Step 2: Cable the strips together in a one to one joining (cabling or weaving are other terms for joining) from bottom to top, alternating the colors. To do this, place two strips side by side on a flat surface, making sure each strip has the beginning knot end at the bottom, and the last loop end at the top. In this way, you can make adjustments to the number of loops fairly easily. Work on the right side of the lace. Working from

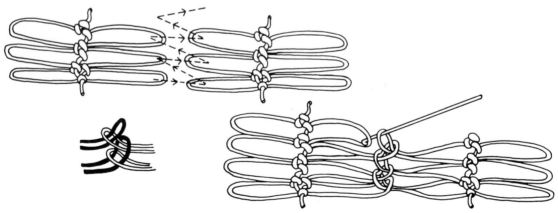

Illus. 50. One to one joining or cabling.

22

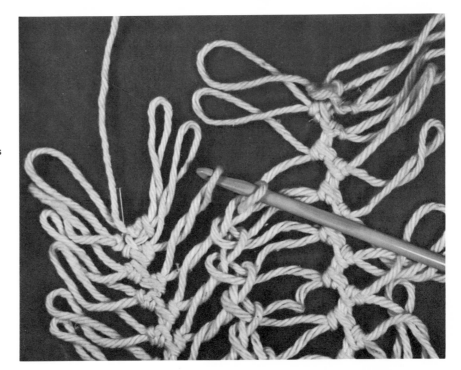

Illus. 51. These two strips are joined by one to one cabling. Notice that you can maintain the twist as you work.

bottom to top, insert the crochet hook into the first loop on the left-hand strip, reach with the hook for the first loop on the right-hand strip and pull it through the left one on the hook (see Illus. 50).

Step 3: Proceed, alternating sides, pulling loops through, in the manner shown in Illus. 51. This one to one joining pattern may be varied by using two or three loops at a time, especially if you are fastening a longer strip to a shorter one. Continually check on the back side to be sure you have not skipped any loops.

Step 4: When you reach the end, work the tail end of yarn (left when you fastened off the sc center) through the last loop to prevent it from unlooping backwards.

Step 5: Following the same procedure, join all five strips together. You may notice a twist in the loops as they rest on a flat surface. You add additional charm to the lace by encouraging and maintaining this twist as you join the strips.

Step 6: Pass six of the pieces of veneer vertically through the rows of loops on both sides of the two outside and center strips.

Step 7: Finish off by latticing the additional strips of wood at the top and bottom (see Illus. 52).

Step 8: Staple the latticed veneer strips together and use a piece of rawhide for a hanger at the top.

Step 9: You may hang ceramic beads strung on lengths of hemp from the bottom.

Use this same technique on a larger scale for decorative and unusual room dividers, screens or window curtains. If you do not insert the veneer strips, the five Hairpin Lace strips cabled together make wonderful place mats for your patio.

Illus. 52. Cover up that bare spot on your wall with a rustic-looking wall hanging which is sure to catch the eye—and admiration—of all your guests.

Illus. 53. To make a colorful beret to top off any outfit, just follow the simple instructions on page 40.

Illus. 54. Choose lively yarns and contrasting lining for a decorative throw pillow for any room.

25

Flower Plaque

Hairpin Lace flowers are so lovely that you will undoubtedly think of many ways in which to display them—in decorations, corsages, trimmings and a wall plaque as in Illus. 40. You can even make Christmas tree ornaments of metallic threads in the round flower-like form.

Materials: straw materials; raffia; sisal; metallic cordings; other firm or stiff materials.

Large flowers result from wide-set frames and small ones from narrow-set frames. Be sure to use crochet hooks of the proper size for the diameter of the yarn or thread you choose. The plaque in Illus. 40 has an assortment of differently shaped flowers.

Add further originality by making other center stitches for the strips than the single crochet center (see page 18). One possibility is the simple chain center, pictured in Illus. 55. Begin as you did for the sc center with a loop round the frame and a knot in the center. Instead of inserting the hook under the loop, however, simply do a chain stitch. Rotate the frame and form a new loop, the same as in Step 2 on page 18. Again, do a chain stitch, using the supply thread. Always make your stitches in front of the prong left of the center knot.

Another possible center stitch is the double braid stitch in Illus. 56. This is a simple variation

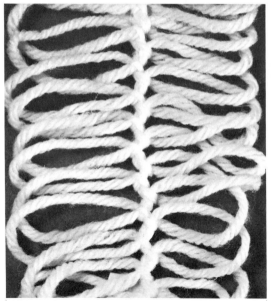

Illus. 55. Hairpin Lace with a chain center.

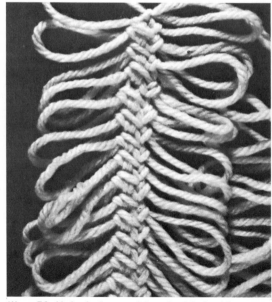

Illus. 56. Hairpin Lace with a double braid center.

of the sc center, for which you pick up both sides —front and back—of the left loop when you pick up the thread with the hook (see Illus. 57). For a sc center, remember, you only pick up the front strand on the left loop. Continue with Steps 2 and 3 of the sc center, always picking up both loops instead of only one (see page 18).

Flat Flowers

Step 1: Set the frame at $1\frac{1}{2}''$ to make a $3''$ flower. Work 20 loops, both sides, with a single crochet center. More than 20 loops at this frame setting results in a rippled flower.

Step 2: Before removing the loops from the frame, run a sturdy thread up through the loops on one side only. Use this to pull up the center after removing the lace from the frame. Tie the thread in a square knot to make a circle. Use the end threads to close the gap where sc meets sc. Fasten off with a hook or needle.

Cone-Shaped Flowers

Raffia is not very long, so if you use it here, tie several strands together first. The flower on the right in Illus. 39 has alternating colors of raffia tied together.

Step 1: Set the frame at $4''$. Make 24 loops of single raffia, both sides.

Step 2: Run a piece of yarn through the loops on one side only. Remove the lace from the frame and pull the yarn up tightly, fastening as you did for the flat flower.

Step 3: For the center, make one 15-loop strip of double yarn or raffia (two colors) on a frame set at $2''$. Set the frame at $1''$ and make a 12-loop strip. Pull a strong thread through one side of the

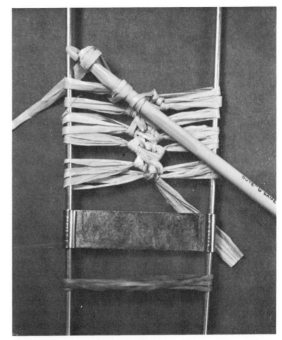

Illus. 57. For the double braid center, pick up both the front and back of the left-of-center loop.

loops of both of these strips to shape them into cones. You may cut the outside loops of the smaller strip, after pulling it into a cone, to make a fuzzy center.

Step 4: Superimpose the three sizes of flowers and, using the end threads, fasten them together at the center.

Stems

Use an 18-gauge uncovered floral wire to make stems like those in Illus. 39. Make a small hook at one end of the wire and pass the wire down from

27

Illus. 58. Close-up of the poncho whose instructions are on pages 40—43.

the flower center (through the tie hole) to form a stem. You can wrap the wire stem with green floral tape. Wire flat corsage flowers in this same manner.

The stems on the plaque in Illus. 40 are simply a row of chain stitches.

Leaves

To make leaves, sc 8-, 12-, and 14-loop green strips, on frame settings of less width than the flowers. Pass a piece of yarn through one side of the strip before removing it from the frame. Pull the yarn only until you form an oblong shape, round at one end and flat at the other. After you have made as many leaves as you want, assemble the plaque. Use a casein-type (white) glue to fasten the flowers to the background. Then glue the stems in place with the leaves.

Illus. 59. You will probably want to buy your pants too big so that you can wear snazzy Hairpin Lace suspenders to hold them up!

Useful All-Round Creations

Throw Pillow

Materials: one 20″ pillow (foam or stuffed) for inside the Hairpin Lace cover; one 4-oz. skein of 4-ply knitting worsted, color A; one 4-oz. skein of 4-ply knitting worsted, color B; Hairpin Lace frame, set at 4″; size H (plastic) or size 0 (metal) crochet hook; tapestry needle.

The colorful pillow in Illus. 54 consists of two sides of four strips each. Make the strips as follows:

Step 1: Strip 1. With color A, make a strip of 30 loops, both sides, with a single crochet center. Before removing the strip from the frame, pass an 8″-length of yarn through the loops on one side only. After removing the lace from the frame, pull it up into a circle, and tie as you did for the flower on page 27. Use the starting and ending threads to secure the sc center of the lace at the circle meeting.

Step 2: Strip 2. With color B, make a strip of 60 loops, both sides. Remove the strip from the frame. Join the two strips with an H crochet hook, starting at the bottom of Strip 2 and at the joining at the circle center of Strip 1. Cable one loop of the center circle of Strip 1 to two loops of Strip 2. When you join unequal numbers of loops together in this way, you "work out the loop." In this case, you join one loop to two loops, but you could also fasten any other unequal number. Illus. 60 shows how you would join six lace loops of color A to nine lace loops of color B. The method is basically the same as for one to one joining

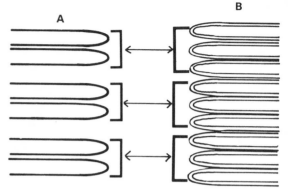

Illus. 60. "Working out the loop" means joining an unequal number of loops. Here is how to join six loops of A to nine loops of B.

(page 22), except that instead of only picking up one loop, pick up as many as your pattern calls for. For the pillow strips, pick up two loops of color B to join to one loop of color A. Work counter-clockwise. Upon completion of the circle, tie the center of Strip 2 on the wrong side.

Step 3: Strip 3. With color A, make a strip of 120 loops, both sides. Remove the strip from the frame. Join Strip 3 to Strip 2, cabling one loop of Strip 2 to two loops of Strip 3 as described above. Tie the ends at the center of the lace.

Step 4: Strip 4. With color B, make a strip of 240 loops, both sides. Remove the strip from the frame. Join Strip 4 to Strip 3, cabling one loop of Strip 3 to two loops of Strip 4. Finish off the center of the lace as usual.

Step 5: These four rows complete one side of the pillow. Repeat all four rows for the other side of the pillow.

Step 6: To join the two sides together, loop side 1 to side 2 by cabling the loops one to one (see page 22), remembering to slip in the pillow before the sides are closed. Tack the last loop securely with needle and yarn.

Try making this pillow with contrasting black and white strips and a flashy coral lining pillow to add pizazz to your couch.

String Grocery Bag

Make a useful, attractive and ecological tote, like the one in Illus. 41, in which to carry your groceries home from the market.

Materials: adjustable Hairpin Lace frame, set at 3″; size G or H crochet hook; two skeins of cotton rug yarn or heavy cording. The bag in Illus. 41 is made of two different colors, A and B, but you may use all one color.

Step 1: sc four strips of color A—that is, make four strips with a sc center—of 40 loops each, both sides (two strips for each side of the bag).

Step 2: sc four strips of color B of 40 loops each, both sides (two strips for each side of the bag).

Step 3: sc two strips of color B of 120 loops each (for the ends and bottom to connect the two sides).

Step 4: Join the 40-loop strips into two sides by cabling one loop to one loop (see page 22) from the bottom up. Each side consists of four joined strips. If you use two colors, alternate A B A B on each side. Make both sides.

Step 5: sc one row along the bottom edge of each side to prepare for joining the long strips to the bottom.

Step 6: Cable the two long strips together one to one.

Step 7: Then, starting at one corner of one side of the bag, join the long double strip along the edge (one to one) to the bottom. With additional yarn, sc the loops of the long strip to the bottom edge (where you made a row of sc in Step 5). Then, continue on up the other edge, cabling the long strip loops to that edge.

Step 8: Repeat Step 7 on the second side of the bag, thus joining all the strips together into the bag.

To finish the open top, follow these steps:

Row 1: sc around the open edge. Close sc row with 3 ch (see page 13—remember that you must make a certain number of chain stitches at the end of every row).

Row 2: dc around. Close row with 3 ch.

CABLING PATTERN FOR THROW PILLOW
Make two sides and cable together one to one.

Color	A	B	A	B
Number of Loops	30	60	120	240
Sequence of Cabling	1 ⟶	2/1 ⟶	2/1 ⟶	2

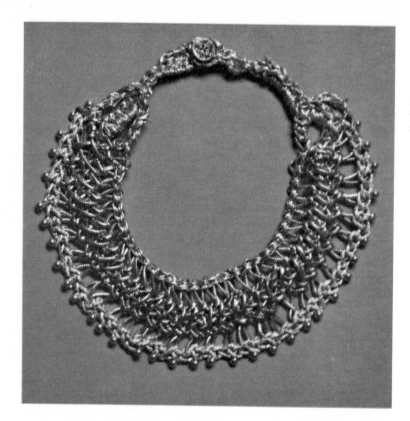

Illus. 61. Instant glamour: Add this necklace to a simple dress and suddenly you have an elegant evening outfit.

Illus. 62. Once you learn the Hairpin Lace technique, you will surely want to make longer and longer strips. Join the strips together into a lovely, comfortable afghan such as this one.

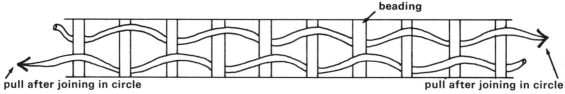

beading

pull after joining in circle   pull after joining in circle

Illus. 63. Weave two pull cords through the beading you have made for an effective and attractive closing for the grocery bag.

Row 3 (beading for the pull cord): Do one dc * ch 3, skip 2 dc on previous row, make 1 dc in next stitch. Repeat from * thus making holes for the pull cord. Close row with 1 ch.

Row 4: sc around. Close row with 1 ch.

Row 5: ch around to finish off top edge.

To make the pull cords, use two one-yard lengths of heavy cording or chain two one-yard cords of cotton yarn. Weave the cords through the holes at the top, one clock-wise and the other counter-clockwise, with the ends at opposite sides of the bag (see Illus. 63). Join the ends on the right and left sides. Pull them away from each other to close the bag (Illus. 63).

If you wish to make a larger bag, with more side strips, be sure to increase the length of the two long strips accordingly. Also, make the side strips proportionately longer for a larger bag.

Tree Mobile

Try the 9-inch-high ornament in Illus. 64 for Christmas.

Materials: adjustable Hairpin Lace frame; 4-ply knitting worsted or metallic thread, use either one or try the two together; size G crochet hook; sequins; casein (white or Elmer's) glue; 2″ of gold cord; a few bright beads; 18-gauge wire, 9″ long.

Step 1: Set the frame at its widest opening (4″).

Leave a long end of yarn at the start. Using a double braid center pattern (see page 26), work 12 loops, both sides, at the 4″ setting.

Step 2: Reset the frame to $3\frac{1}{2}″$ and work nine loops, both sides.

Step 3: Reset the frame to 3″ and work six loops, both sides.

Step 4: Reset the frame to 2″ and work five loops, both sides.

Step 5: Reset the frame to $1\frac{1}{2}″$ and work four loops, both sides. This process makes a tapered piece of lace. Leave a long piece of yarn for a hanger at the top. The lace twists when you remove it from the frame; encourage this for a special three-dimensional effect.

Step 6: Run wire up through the center of the braid from the bottom to the top to stiffen your tree. Glue sequins on the loops' ends.

Step 7: Thread gold cord in a needle and run it up from the bottom to the top, covering the wire, and down the other side of the braid center, also covering the wire on that side.

Hang beads on the bottom as in Illus. 64 for a finishing touch which also adds stability to the bottom.

Illus. 64. Here is a handsome tree ornament that will not break when it falls.

Expand Your Wardrobe

Ribbon Belt

Follow this simple pattern for the yellow belt in Illus. 66. The materials and instructions here are for a 34″ belt. Be sure to make adjustments for larger or smaller sizes.

Materials: one ball of ornamental crochet cotton thread with a metallic twist, any color; Hairpin Lace frame set at 1″; two yards of ¼″ grosgrain ribbon and a long-eye needle; one pearl or metal buckle with a 1″ slot; felt or soft leather of a shade related to the thread and ribbon for the buckle end and tip.

Step 1: Work a strip of 130 loops, both sides, using the sc center stitch. This piece of lace has some stretch.

Step 2: Before removing the lace from the frame, thread the ¼″ grosgrain ribbon onto the needle and pass it down one side, through the loops and up the other side through those loops. Remove the whole thing from the frame and adjust the ribbon evenly.

Step 3: Cut two pieces of felt in an elongated diamond shape for the belt tip (Illus. 65). Be sure to cut the felt the width of the belt.

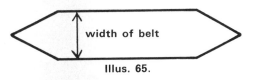

width of belt

Illus. 65.

Step 4: Stitch, preferably on a sewing machine, but by hand if a machine is unavailable, one piece of felt on the inside and one on the outside of the

35

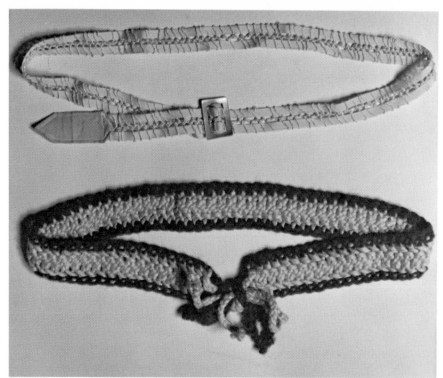

Illus. 66. Belts are in! Make thin ones, wide ones, fancy ones, tie ones, buckle ones— the possibilities are innumerable with Hairpin Lace.

belt, covering the ends of the ribbon and catching the first loop of the Hairpin Lace (see belt tip in Illus. 66). Trim even if necessary.

Step 5: Cut two pieces of felt the width of the belt and 2″ long. Stitch the felt pieces together, again preferably by machine, over the buckle end of the belt, catching the last loop inside. Pass this felt end through the buckle and hand tack it securely in place.

Bulky Belt

For a different, more casual look, make a bulky belt like the brown one shown in Illus. 66. The materials and instructions are for a belt 33″ long.

Materials: two colors of cotton rug yarn, one for the body of the belt and the other for the edging; size 00 crochet hook; Hairpin Lace frame, set at $1\frac{1}{2}$″; tapestry needle.

Step 1: Work 82 loops, both sides, with sc center stitch. Remove the lace from the frame. With the needle, work in the thread ends.

Step 2: sc an edge round the lace with a contrasting color (see bottom edge in Illus. 67 for loops single crocheted together), by just inserting your hook in each loop and proceeding as usual for sc. Leave the two holes at each end between the center sc and the edge sc. Work the ends in with the needle.

Step 3: ch two 24″ lengths for ties, one of one color and the second of the other color. Work the thread ends securely back into the chain. Pass the ties through the holes of the belt to tie at the waist.

Suspenders

Materials: one skein cotton crochet thread (white in Illus. 59); two colors of sisal for edging (red and blue in Illus. 59); one set of three suspender clips; size 00 crochet hook; Hairpin Lace frame, set at 1″.

Step 1: Using double braid center (see page 26), work one strip 38″ long and one strip 44″ long, in white. Leave 10″ ends.

Step 2: sc sisal along the long edges, using one color on one side and the second color on the other side. Leave 10″ ends.

Step 3: With the end threads, fasten the two strips together in a "Y" at the 38″ point by weaving the threads into the crocheted strip. Leave a 6″ end, the base of the "Y," to fasten in the center back of the pants (see Illus. 68).

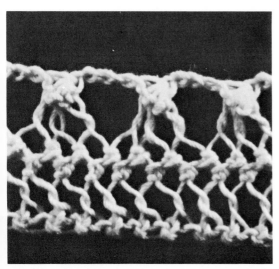

Illus. 67. The lower edge shows loops single crocheted together; the upper edge shows three loops crocheted together with chain 3 between.

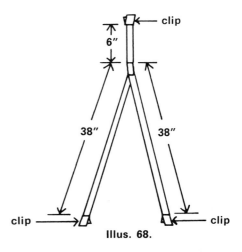

Illus. 68.

37

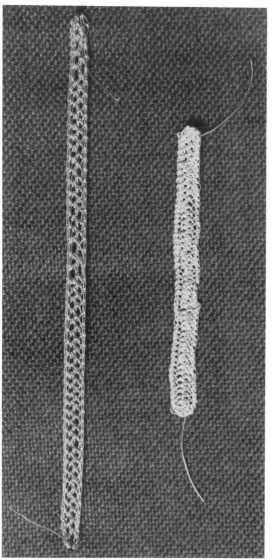

Step 4: Fasten each one of the suspender clips to each one of the three ends with the end threads. Work the back in and glue with a type of white glue/paste called "Tacky White Glue" or with Elmer's Glue.

These suspenders have some give, but if more is needed for length, stitch a 3″ piece of elastic at the base of the "Y." Use silver elastic thread for glamorous suspenders, hat bands or hugging belts. Work the elastic loosely and sc along the edges. The completed item will stretch double. The two belts in Illus. 69 are actually the same length, but the one on the left has been stretched to just about twice its original length.

For another unusual touch, you might add an elaborately finished edge such as the one in Illus. 70. First sc 3 loops together with ch 6 between, ending with sc of the last three loops together. Then, ch 6, 1 sc around the ch 6 (at about the midpoint) from the previous row. Repeat for one more row.

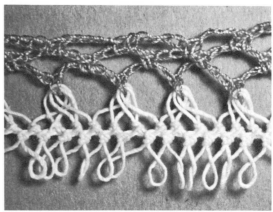

Illus. 69. If you are unsure of size, make stretch-able elastic belts such as these.

Illus. 70. An elaborate edge changes the whole look of any Hairpin Lace project.

Necklace of Metallic Thread

Materials: Hairpin Lace frame, set at 2″; size G crochet hook; three sizes of gold or silver cording—heavy, medium and fine; 34 gold or silver beads with holes large enough to carry the fine cording; one gold or silver button.

The gauge for the length of the cording is: one yard of cord equals four loops, both sides, at a 2″ frame setting.

Step 1: Work 33 loops, both sides, with the double braid center stitch (see page 26), leaving 6″ ends of cord on both ends.

Step 2: With the medium cording, sc loops together (see page 37) on one edge, which then becomes the neck edge.

Step 3: On the opposite edge—now the outside edge—do one sc in the first loop with heavy cording, * ch 1, sc in next loop. Repeat from * across the lower edge, thus increasing the width.

Step 4: String the 34 beads on the fine cording which is still connected to the ball. On the outside edge * sc in the first sc of the previous row, move up one bead on the thread, sc in ch on the previous row. Repeat from * to the end of the necklace, using all the beads. Work the ends of the fine cording back into the crocheted edge. The beads lie flat on the outside of each Hairpin loop.

Step 5: You now have a semi-circular necklace with three long cord ends protruding from each end. Work these into the center of the Hairpin Lace so that all the ends are bunched in the middle and stick straight out at each end (see Illus. 71). These will form the fastening part of the necklace.

Step 6: Using this bundle as a core, fasten the medium weight cord to the body of the necklace

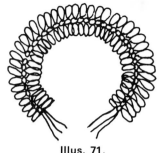

Illus. 71.

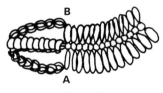

Illus. 72.

and sc tightly around these bunched ends, covering them from the neck edge outward. After each end measures about 4″, ch a loop for buttoning at one end and a flat area on which to sew the button at the other.

Step 7: In order to make this closing more graceful, join the medium weight cord at the base of each end and chain from corner A to the covered core center and back to corner B (see Illus. 72). This makes a triangle fastening the ends of the necklace together.

Step 8: Work any loose ends in with the hook and glue flat with white glue/paste called "Tacky White Glue" or with Elmer's Glue.

Sew on a decorative button to complete this original necklace, pictured on page 32.

Beret

Materials: homespun yarn, either commercial or hand-made—3 oz. color A and 3 oz. color B (white and brown in Illus. 53); adjustable Hairpin Lace frame; size H crochet hook.

Make the first three strips of the beret in Illus. 53 in the same way as the pillow on page 30.

Step 1: Set the frame at 3″. Strip 1. Make 30 loops, both sides, with color A. Pull up into a circle as on page 27.

Step 2: Strip 2. Make 60 loops, both sides, with color B. Cable Strip 1 (circle) to Strip 2 in a one loop to two loop sequence—one loop of Strip 1 to two loops of Strip 2—counter-clockwise (see page 30).

Step 3: Strip 3. With color A, make 120 loops, both sides. Cable Strip 2 to Strip 3 in a one loop to two loop sequence (see page 30), counter-clockwise.

Step 4: Strip 4. With this strip, the beret begins to turn in towards the head. Set the frame at 2″. With color B, make 60 loops, both sides. Cable Strip 3 to Strip 4 in a two loop to one loop sequence—two loops of Strip 3 to one loop of Strip 4. The outside edge has a soft, rippling appearance.

Step 5: Keep the frame set at 2″. With color A, make 60 loops, both sides. Cable Strip 5 to Strip 4 in a one to one sequence.

Step 6: Finish the inner edge of the beret with one row of dc in color B.

Make a 2″ or 3″ pompom of mixed A and B yarn for the top of the beret. To do this, wrap (loop) A and B round a 2″- or 3″-wide piece of cardboard. The more times you wrap the yarn, the fuller the pompom will be. When you have wound enough yarn, slide it off the cardboard, tie a firm knot around the middle of the yarn loops, cut the looped edges and fluff the pompom. Attach it to the beret.

Poncho

The following instructions are for the poncho in Illus. 58 which will fit sizes 12, 14 and 16.

Materials: 3-ply worsted wool, colors A, B and C (white, red and blue), 6 oz. of each; adjustable Hairpin Lace frame, set at 2″, or a fixed 2″-frame; size G crochet hook; needle and safety pins.

A time-saving tip for this poncho—as well as for any projects with long strips—is to mark each 25 stitches with a safety pin to facilitate counting. Also, mark your frame on the front side with a felt-tip marker, so you know when the front is towards you. Then, you know that both sides have the same number of loops on them.

Scale: 4 loops per 1″.

Step 1: Use the double braid center and work 17 strips for each side. Leave long ends at each end of each strip. Mark the center of each strip with a safety pin as you work. If you make errors in counting, you can fairly easily adjust the loops at the shoulders.

Strip 1-A (white). Work 48 loops, both sides. Mark the center between loops 24 and 25 with a pin.

Strip 2-B (red). Work 68 loops, both sides. Mark the center between loops 34 and 35.

Strip 3-C (blue). Work 88 loops, both sides. Mark the center between loops 44 and 45.

Strip 4-A (white). Work 108 loops, both sides. Mark the center between loops 54 and 55.

Strip 5-B (red). Work 128 loops, both sides. Mark the center between loops 64 and 65.

Strip 6-C (blue). Work 148 loops, both sides. Mark the center between loops 74 and 75.

Strip 7-A (white). Work 168 loops, both sides. Mark the center between loops 84 and 85.

Strip 8-B (red). Work 188 loops, both sides. Mark the center between loops 94 and 95.

Strip 9-C (blue). Work 208 loops, both sides. Mark the center between loops 104 and 105.

Continue this same pattern, increasing 5″ or 20 loops each strip and dividing them equally either side of the center mark. If this flares too much to suit you, decrease the number of increased loops from 20 to 10.

Step 2: To cable the strips together, avoid having to straighten and untwist each strip later by cabling each strip to the one above it at the time of completion. Mark the front right side and the back right side, so you always work on the right side. Start cabling at the center each time. Work first to the right from the center to the shoulder and then to the left from the center to the shoulder. Work on a large flat area to avoid skipping loops and to encourage the "V" at the front center.

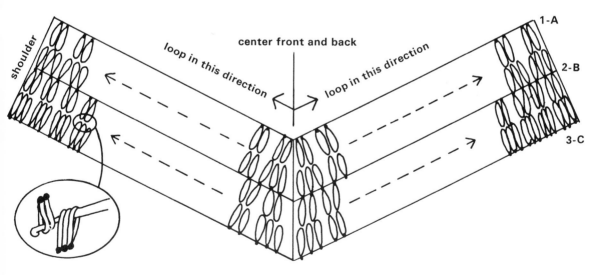

Illus. 73. Cabling pattern for the poncho.

Strip 1-A   to   *Strip 2-B*
(working from the center to the right shoulder)

2 loops	to	3 loops
2 loops	to	2 loops
2 loops	to	2 loops

Continue this system until there are 6 loops remaining on Strip 2-B, then do:

2 loops	to	3 loops
2 loops	to	3 loops

Repeat this pattern from the center, working to the left shoulder.

Strip 2-B   to   *Strip 3-C*

2 loops	to	3 loops
2 loops	to	2 loops
2 loops	to	2 loops

Continue this system until there are 12 loops remaining on 3-C, then do:

2 loops	to	3 loops
2 loops	to	3 loops
2 loops	to	3 loops
2 loops	to	3 loops

Repeat from the center to the left shoulder.

Strip 3-C   to   *Strip 4-A*

2 loops	to	3 loops

2 loops	to	3 loops
2 loops	to	2 loops
2 loops	to	2 loops

Continue this system until there are 12 loops remaining on 4-A, then do:

2 loops	to	3 loops
2 loops	to	3 loops
2 loops	to	3 loops
2 loops	to	3 loops

Repeat from the center to the left shoulder.

Strip 4-A   to   *Strip 5-B*

2 loops	to	3 loops
2 loops	to	3 loops
2 loops	to	2 loops
2 loops	to	2 loops

Continue this system until there are 12 loops remaining on 5-B, then do:

2 loops	to	3 loops
2 loops	to	3 loops
2 loops	to	3 loops
2 loops	to	3 loops

Repeat from the center to the left shoulder.

Continue this system through the 17 rows or to the length you wish. If you choose to decrease the increase in width by one half (from 20 loops to 10), the pattern remains the same.

Step 3: Before assembling the two sides of the poncho, finish each neck edge separately. The reason for this is that you may wish to put buttons on one or both shoulders for warmth and fit round the neck.

Row 1: Loosely sc the neck edge, turn, ch 3.

Row 2: Do shell stitch on return row. Use the same shell stitch as you did for the handkerchief on page 20.

Step 4: To assemble both sides together: sc along the edges from the neck at the shoulder to the bottom edge or each side—front and back—to give a firmness (four times in all).

Step 5: At this point, you have a choice: If you wish to minimize the side seam, whip these crocheted edges together with an over and over stitch with a needle and yarn on the wrong side. If you wish to emphasize the joining as part of the design, work a row of dc after the sc on each edge and whip them together. This will make a band down the shoulder seam.

Make a matching beret for your poncho, following the instructions on page 40.

Be original and try a skirt of heavy, firm wool or cotton yarn, in colored strips similar to those you made for the poncho, setting your frame at its widest setting, or making your own frame of the desired width.

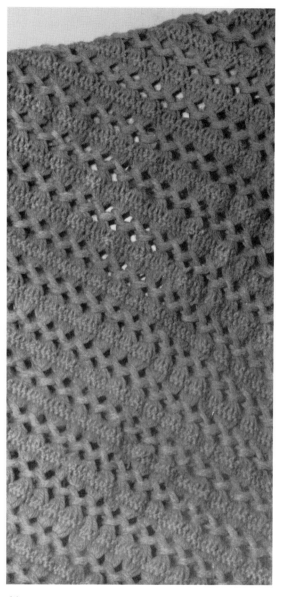

Think Big

Shawls, Stoles and Afghans

If you want to make a shawl or stole like the one on the front cover or an afghan like the one in Illus. 62, first make yourself an extra long—but not longer than 18″—Hairpin Lace frame. To make such a long frame, use a long set of metal knitting needles about size 8 (English size 5), or use welding rods of about this same diameter. Cut the heads off the knitting needles and smooth the ends. Cut two pieces of $\frac{1}{2}$″ dowelling $4\frac{1}{2}$″ long, and two pieces $3\frac{1}{2}$″ long. Drill holes the diameter of the needles 4″ apart and 3″ apart respectively on the two sets of dowelling. This provides two separate Hairpin Lace frames for long strips of lace.

Make Hairpin Lace as you have learned, of a length you select and with a center stitch of your choice. As you make the lace, mark your stitches and the frame as indicated on page 40.

When removing already-made lace from a frame to continue longer lengths, use a knitting holder, as long as you can find. By placing the loops of one side on the holder, you protect the lace from twisting and taking extra time to straighten when you cable the strips together.

Illus. 74. Close-up of the Hairpin Lace afghan shown on page 33. Choose joining and center stitch patterns according to your own creative taste.

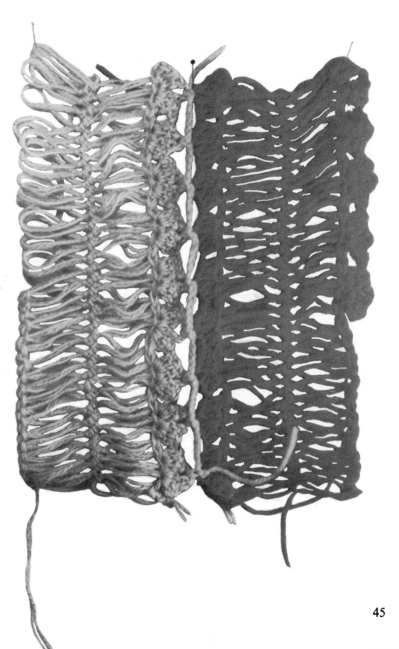

Illus. 75. For this edging, chain together two strips that each have a shell stitch edging. Imagine any of several uses for this attractive finishing touch.

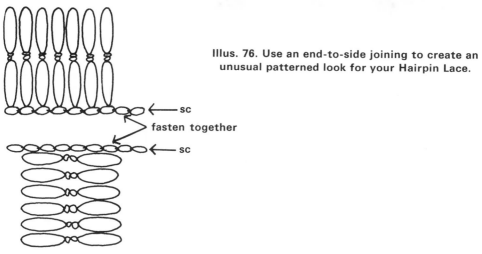

Illus. 76. Use an end-to-side joining to create an unusual patterned look for your Hairpin Lace.

← sc

fasten together

← sc

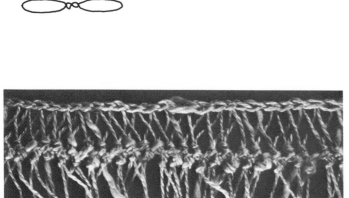

Illus. 77. Hairpin Lace fringe is really easy to make. Simply cut open the loops on the outside edge of your project.

Always cable the long strips together from the bottom (beginning) to the top (ending) to allow for adjustment of the numbers of loops. It is sometimes hard to work the proper number of loops when it is in the hundreds.

The charm of an unusual stole or shawl is in the method of cabling the Hairpin strips together. One to one is usual, but grouping the loops in threes and fours makes a lacier finished product.

In addition, a crocheted edging on each side of the Hairpin Lace loops is most attractive and has a charm all its own. One such possible pattern is the shell edging shown in Illus. 75. Another type of joining is an end-to-side joining, pictured in Illus. 76. For this, sc the loops of one end of the strip together and sc the loops along the side of the other strip. Then, sc the two rows of sc to each other.

An attractive way to finish the edge of a shawl or afghan is to make fringe of Hairpin Lace. Work a strip of the length necessary for the fringe. Cable the strip onto the body of the afghan or stole. Either leave the second side of the fringe in loops or cut it, as in Illus. 77, for open fringe.

Try making a bedspread as you would an afghan, using a contrasting bright lining and a lacy joining. As you can see, with a little imagination, you can use Hairpin Lace in an endless number of unique projects.

Index